This Jewelry Making Log Book belongs to:

_____

DEDICATION

This Jewelry Making Notebook is dedicated to all the Jewelry Lovers out there who love to plan out and design jewelry, and document their findings in the process.

You are my inspiration for producing books and I'm honored to be a part of keeping all of your designs and records organized.

How to use this Jewelry Making Notebook:

This useful jewelry project log book is a must-have for anyone that loves the art of designing jewellery! You will love this easy to use journal to track and record all your architecture activities.

Each interior page includes space to record & track the following:

1. Project Name - Write down the name of the current project.
2. Date - Use this space to fill in the date of the project.
3. Clients - Record and Track the client's name.
4. Budget - Fill in the allowed budget for this project.
5. Deadline - Write out the deadline for the project.
6. Dimensions - Stay on task using the grid graph to sketch out the front, side and top view of the piece of jewelry.
7. Material Components - Write out the details of each material, weight, quantity and the price.

If you are new to the world of making jewelry or have been at it for a while, this jewelry making planner is a must have! Can make a great useful gift for anyone that loves to make jewelry!

Have Fun!

PROJECT

FRONT VIEW

CLIENT

BUDGET

DEADLINE

NOTES

SIDE VIEW

TOP VIEW

MATERIAL COMPONENTS

MATERIALS	WEIGHT	QUANTITY	PRICE

PROJECT

FRONT VIEW

CLIENT

BUDGET

DEADLINE

NOTES

SIDE VIEW

TOP VIEW

MATERIAL COMPONENTS

MATERIALS	WEIGHT	QUANTITY	PRICE

PROJECT

FRONT VIEW

CLIENT

BUDGET

DEADLINE

NOTES

SIDE VIEW

TOP VIEW

MATERIAL COMPONENTS

MATERIALS	WEIGHT	QUANTITY	PRICE

PROJECT

FRONT VIEW

CLIENT

BUDGET

DEADLINE

NOTES

SIDE VIEW

TOP VIEW

MATERIAL COMPONENTS

MATERIALS	WEIGHT	QUANTITY	PRICE

PROJECT

FRONT VIEW

CLIENT

BUDGET

DEADLINE

NOTES

SIDE VIEW

TOP VIEW

MATERIAL COMPONENTS

MATERIALS	WEIGHT	QUANTITY	PRICE

PROJECT

FRONT VIEW

CLIENT

BUDGET

DEADLINE

NOTES

SIDE VIEW

TOP VIEW

MATERIAL COMPONENTS

MATERIALS	WEIGHT	QUANTITY	PRICE

PROJECT

FRONT VIEW

- CLIENT
- BUDGET
- DEADLINE

NOTES

SIDE VIEW

TOP VIEW

MATERIAL COMPONENTS

MATERIALS	WEIGHT	QUANTITY	PRICE

PROJECT

FRONT VIEW

CLIENT

BUDGET

DEADLINE

NOTES

SIDE VIEW

TOP VIEW

MATERIAL COMPONENTS

MATERIALS	WEIGHT	QUANTITY	PRICE

PROJECT

FRONT VIEW

CLIENT

BUDGET

DEADLINE

NOTES

SIDE VIEW

TOP VIEW

MATERIAL COMPONENTS

MATERIALS	WEIGHT	QUANTITY	PRICE

PROJECT

FRONT VIEW

CLIENT

BUDGET

DEADLINE

NOTES

SIDE VIEW

TOP VIEW

MATERIAL COMPONENTS

MATERIALS	WEIGHT	QUANTITY	PRICE

PROJECT

FRONT VIEW

CLIENT

BUDGET

DEADLINE

NOTES

SIDE VIEW

TOP VIEW

MATERIAL COMPONENTS

MATERIALS	WEIGHT	QUANTITY	PRICE

PROJECT

FRONT VIEW

- CLIENT
- BUDGET
- DEADLINE

NOTES

SIDE VIEW

TOP VIEW

MATERIAL COMPONENTS

MATERIALS	WEIGHT	QUANTITY	PRICE

PROJECT

FRONT VIEW

CLIENT

BUDGET

DEADLINE

NOTES

SIDE VIEW

TOP VIEW

MATERIAL COMPONENTS

MATERIALS	WEIGHT	QUANTITY	PRICE

PROJECT

FRONT VIEW

CLIENT

BUDGET

DEADLINE

NOTES

SIDE VIEW

TOP VIEW

MATERIAL COMPONENTS

MATERIALS	WEIGHT	QUANTITY	PRICE

PROJECT

FRONT VIEW

CLIENT

BUDGET

DEADLINE

NOTES

SIDE VIEW

TOP VIEW

MATERIAL COMPONENTS

MATERIALS	WEIGHT	QUANTITY	PRICE

PROJECT

FRONT VIEW

CLIENT	
BUDGET	
DEADLINE	

NOTES

SIDE VIEW

TOP VIEW

MATERIAL COMPONENTS

MATERIALS	WEIGHT	QUANTITY	PRICE

PROJECT

FRONT VIEW

CLIENT

BUDGET

DEADLINE

NOTES

SIDE VIEW

TOP VIEW

MATERIAL COMPONENTS

MATERIALS	WEIGHT	QUANTITY	PRICE

PROJECT

FRONT VIEW

CLIENT

BUDGET

DEADLINE

NOTES

SIDE VIEW

TOP VIEW

MATERIAL COMPONENTS

MATERIALS	WEIGHT	QUANTITY	PRICE

PROJECT

FRONT VIEW

CLIENT

BUDGET

DEADLINE

NOTES

SIDE VIEW

TOP VIEW

MATERIAL COMPONENTS

MATERIALS	WEIGHT	QUANTITY	PRICE

PROJECT

FRONT VIEW

CLIENT

BUDGET

DEADLINE

NOTES

SIDE VIEW

TOP VIEW

MATERIAL COMPONENTS

MATERIALS	WEIGHT	QUANTITY	PRICE

PROJECT

FRONT VIEW

CLIENT

BUDGET

DEADLINE

NOTES

SIDE VIEW

TOP VIEW

MATERIAL COMPONENTS

MATERIALS	WEIGHT	QUANTITY	PRICE

PROJECT

FRONT VIEW

CLIENT

BUDGET

DEADLINE

NOTES

SIDE VIEW

TOP VIEW

MATERIAL COMPONENTS

MATERIALS	WEIGHT	QUANTITY	PRICE

PROJECT

FRONT VIEW

CLIENT

BUDGET

DEADLINE

NOTES

SIDE VIEW

TOP VIEW

MATERIAL COMPONENTS

MATERIALS	WEIGHT	QUANTITY	PRICE

PROJECT

FRONT VIEW

CLIENT

BUDGET

DEADLINE

NOTES

SIDE VIEW

TOP VIEW

MATERIAL COMPONENTS

MATERIALS	WEIGHT	QUANTITY	PRICE

PROJECT

FRONT VIEW

CLIENT

BUDGET

DEADLINE

NOTES

SIDE VIEW

TOP VIEW

MATERIAL COMPONENTS

MATERIALS	WEIGHT	QUANTITY	PRICE

PROJECT

FRONT VIEW

- CLIENT
- BUDGET
- DEADLINE

NOTES

SIDE VIEW

TOP VIEW

MATERIAL COMPONENTS

MATERIALS	WEIGHT	QUANTITY	PRICE

PROJECT

FRONT VIEW

CLIENT

BUDGET

DEADLINE

NOTES

SIDE VIEW

TOP VIEW

MATERIAL COMPONENTS

MATERIALS	WEIGHT	QUANTITY	PRICE

PROJECT

FRONT VIEW

CLIENT

BUDGET

DEADLINE

NOTES

SIDE VIEW

TOP VIEW

MATERIAL COMPONENTS

MATERIALS	WEIGHT	QUANTITY	PRICE

PROJECT

FRONT VIEW

CLIENT

BUDGET

DEADLINE

NOTES

SIDE VIEW

TOP VIEW

MATERIAL COMPONENTS

MATERIALS	WEIGHT	QUANTITY	PRICE

PROJECT

FRONT VIEW

CLIENT

BUDGET

DEADLINE

NOTES

SIDE VIEW

TOP VIEW

MATERIAL COMPONENTS

MATERIALS	WEIGHT	QUANTITY	PRICE

PROJECT

FRONT VIEW

- CLIENT
- BUDGET
- DEADLINE

NOTES

SIDE VIEW

TOP VIEW

MATERIAL COMPONENTS

MATERIALS	WEIGHT	QUANTITY	PRICE

PROJECT

FRONT VIEW

CLIENT

BUDGET

DEADLINE

NOTES

SIDE VIEW

TOP VIEW

MATERIAL COMPONENTS

MATERIALS	WEIGHT	QUANTITY	PRICE

PROJECT

FRONT VIEW

CLIENT

BUDGET

DEADLINE

NOTES

SIDE VIEW

TOP VIEW

MATERIAL COMPONENTS

MATERIALS	WEIGHT	QUANTITY	PRICE

PROJECT

FRONT VIEW

CLIENT

BUDGET

DEADLINE

NOTES

SIDE VIEW

TOP VIEW

MATERIAL COMPONENTS

MATERIALS	WEIGHT	QUANTITY	PRICE

PROJECT

FRONT VIEW

CLIENT

BUDGET

DEADLINE

NOTES

SIDE VIEW

TOP VIEW

MATERIAL COMPONENTS

MATERIALS	WEIGHT	QUANTITY	PRICE

PROJECT

FRONT VIEW

CLIENT

BUDGET

DEADLINE

NOTES

SIDE VIEW

TOP VIEW

MATERIAL COMPONENTS

MATERIALS	WEIGHT	QUANTITY	PRICE

PROJECT

FRONT VIEW

CLIENT

BUDGET

DEADLINE

NOTES

SIDE VIEW

TOP VIEW

MATERIAL COMPONENTS

MATERIALS	WEIGHT	QUANTITY	PRICE

PROJECT

FRONT VIEW

CLIENT

BUDGET

DEADLINE

NOTES

SIDE VIEW

TOP VIEW

MATERIAL COMPONENTS

MATERIALS	WEIGHT	QUANTITY	PRICE

PROJECT

FRONT VIEW

CLIENT

BUDGET

DEADLINE

NOTES

SIDE VIEW

TOP VIEW

MATERIAL COMPONENTS

MATERIALS	WEIGHT	QUANTITY	PRICE

PROJECT

FRONT VIEW

CLIENT

BUDGET

DEADLINE

NOTES

SIDE VIEW

TOP VIEW

MATERIAL COMPONENTS

MATERIALS	WEIGHT	QUANTITY	PRICE

PROJECT

FRONT VIEW

CLIENT

BUDGET

DEADLINE

NOTES

SIDE VIEW

TOP VIEW

MATERIAL COMPONENTS

MATERIALS	WEIGHT	QUANTITY	PRICE

PROJECT

FRONT VIEW

CLIENT

BUDGET

DEADLINE

NOTES

SIDE VIEW

TOP VIEW

MATERIAL COMPONENTS

MATERIALS	WEIGHT	QUANTITY	PRICE

PROJECT

FRONT VIEW

CLIENT

BUDGET

DEADLINE

NOTES

SIDE VIEW

TOP VIEW

MATERIAL COMPONENTS			
MATERIALS	WEIGHT	QUANTITY	PRICE

PROJECT

FRONT VIEW

CLIENT

BUDGET

DEADLINE

NOTES

SIDE VIEW

TOP VIEW

MATERIAL COMPONENTS

MATERIALS	WEIGHT	QUANTITY	PRICE

PROJECT

FRONT VIEW

CLIENT	
BUDGET	
DEADLINE	

NOTES

SIDE VIEW

TOP VIEW

MATERIAL COMPONENTS

MATERIALS	WEIGHT	QUANTITY	PRICE

PROJECT

FRONT VIEW

CLIENT

BUDGET

DEADLINE

NOTES

SIDE VIEW

TOP VIEW

MATERIAL COMPONENTS

MATERIALS	WEIGHT	QUANTITY	PRICE

PROJECT

FRONT VIEW

CLIENT

BUDGET

DEADLINE

NOTES

SIDE VIEW

TOP VIEW

MATERIAL COMPONENTS

MATERIALS	WEIGHT	QUANTITY	PRICE

PROJECT

FRONT VIEW

- CLIENT
- BUDGET
- DEADLINE

NOTES

SIDE VIEW

TOP VIEW

MATERIAL COMPONENTS

MATERIALS	WEIGHT	QUANTITY	PRICE

PROJECT

FRONT VIEW

CLIENT

BUDGET

DEADLINE

NOTES

SIDE VIEW

TOP VIEW

MATERIAL COMPONENTS

MATERIALS	WEIGHT	QUANTITY	PRICE

PROJECT

FRONT VIEW

- CLIENT
- BUDGET
- DEADLINE

NOTES

SIDE VIEW

TOP VIEW

MATERIAL COMPONENTS

MATERIALS	WEIGHT	QUANTITY	PRICE

PROJECT

FRONT VIEW

CLIENT

BUDGET

DEADLINE

NOTES

SIDE VIEW

TOP VIEW

MATERIAL COMPONENTS

MATERIALS	WEIGHT	QUANTITY	PRICE

PROJECT

FRONT VIEW

- CLIENT
- BUDGET
- DEADLINE

NOTES

SIDE VIEW

TOP VIEW

MATERIAL COMPONENTS

MATERIALS	WEIGHT	QUANTITY	PRICE

PROJECT

FRONT VIEW

CLIENT

BUDGET

DEADLINE

NOTES

SIDE VIEW

TOP VIEW

MATERIAL COMPONENTS

MATERIALS	WEIGHT	QUANTITY	PRICE

PROJECT

FRONT VIEW

CLIENT

BUDGET

DEADLINE

NOTES

SIDE VIEW

TOP VIEW

MATERIAL COMPONENTS

MATERIALS	WEIGHT	QUANTITY	PRICE

PROJECT

FRONT VIEW

- CLIENT
- BUDGET
- DEADLINE

NOTES

SIDE VIEW

TOP VIEW

MATERIAL COMPONENTS

MATERIALS	WEIGHT	QUANTITY	PRICE

PROJECT

FRONT VIEW

- CLIENT
- BUDGET
- DEADLINE

NOTES

SIDE VIEW

TOP VIEW

MATERIAL COMPONENTS

MATERIALS	WEIGHT	QUANTITY	PRICE

PROJECT

FRONT VIEW

CLIENT

BUDGET

DEADLINE

NOTES

SIDE VIEW

TOP VIEW

MATERIAL COMPONENTS

MATERIALS	WEIGHT	QUANTITY	PRICE

PROJECT

FRONT VIEW

CLIENT

BUDGET

DEADLINE

NOTES

SIDE VIEW

TOP VIEW

MATERIAL COMPONENTS

MATERIALS	WEIGHT	QUANTITY	PRICE

PROJECT

FRONT VIEW

CLIENT

BUDGET

DEADLINE

NOTES

SIDE VIEW

TOP VIEW

MATERIAL COMPONENTS

MATERIALS	WEIGHT	QUANTITY	PRICE

PROJECT

FRONT VIEW

CLIENT

BUDGET

DEADLINE

NOTES

SIDE VIEW

TOP VIEW

MATERIAL COMPONENTS

MATERIALS	WEIGHT	QUANTITY	PRICE

PROJECT

FRONT VIEW

- CLIENT
- BUDGET
- DEADLINE

NOTES

SIDE VIEW

TOP VIEW

MATERIAL COMPONENTS

MATERIALS	WEIGHT	QUANTITY	PRICE

PROJECT

FRONT VIEW

- CLIENT
- BUDGET
- DEADLINE

NOTES

SIDE VIEW

TOP VIEW

MATERIAL COMPONENTS

MATERIALS	WEIGHT	QUANTITY	PRICE

PROJECT

FRONT VIEW

CLIENT

BUDGET

DEADLINE

NOTES

SIDE VIEW

TOP VIEW

MATERIAL COMPONENTS

MATERIALS	WEIGHT	QUANTITY	PRICE

PROJECT

FRONT VIEW

CLIENT

BUDGET

DEADLINE

NOTES

SIDE VIEW

TOP VIEW

MATERIAL COMPONENTS

MATERIALS	WEIGHT	QUANTITY	PRICE

PROJECT

FRONT VIEW

CLIENT	
BUDGET	
DEADLINE	

NOTES

SIDE VIEW

TOP VIEW

MATERIAL COMPONENTS

MATERIALS	WEIGHT	QUANTITY	PRICE

PROJECT

FRONT VIEW

CLIENT

BUDGET

DEADLINE

NOTES

SIDE VIEW

TOP VIEW

MATERIAL COMPONENTS

MATERIALS	WEIGHT	QUANTITY	PRICE

PROJECT

FRONT VIEW

CLIENT

BUDGET

DEADLINE

NOTES

SIDE VIEW

TOP VIEW

MATERIAL COMPONENTS

MATERIALS	WEIGHT	QUANTITY	PRICE

PROJECT

FRONT VIEW

CLIENT

BUDGET

DEADLINE

NOTES

SIDE VIEW

TOP VIEW

MATERIAL COMPONENTS

MATERIALS	WEIGHT	QUANTITY	PRICE

PROJECT

FRONT VIEW

CLIENT

BUDGET

DEADLINE

NOTES

SIDE VIEW

TOP VIEW

MATERIAL COMPONENTS

MATERIALS	WEIGHT	QUANTITY	PRICE

PROJECT

FRONT VIEW

CLIENT

BUDGET

DEADLINE

NOTES

SIDE VIEW

TOP VIEW

MATERIAL COMPONENTS

MATERIALS	WEIGHT	QUANTITY	PRICE

PROJECT

FRONT VIEW

- CLIENT
- BUDGET
- DEADLINE

NOTES

SIDE VIEW

TOP VIEW

MATERIAL COMPONENTS

MATERIALS	WEIGHT	QUANTITY	PRICE

PROJECT

FRONT VIEW

CLIENT

BUDGET

DEADLINE

NOTES

SIDE VIEW

TOP VIEW

MATERIAL COMPONENTS

MATERIALS	WEIGHT	QUANTITY	PRICE

PROJECT

FRONT VIEW

CLIENT

BUDGET

DEADLINE

NOTES

SIDE VIEW

TOP VIEW

MATERIAL COMPONENTS

MATERIALS	WEIGHT	QUANTITY	PRICE

PROJECT

FRONT VIEW

CLIENT

BUDGET

DEADLINE

NOTES

SIDE VIEW

TOP VIEW

MATERIAL COMPONENTS

MATERIALS	WEIGHT	QUANTITY	PRICE

PROJECT

FRONT VIEW

CLIENT

BUDGET

DEADLINE

NOTES

SIDE VIEW

TOP VIEW

MATERIAL COMPONENTS

MATERIALS	WEIGHT	QUANTITY	PRICE

PROJECT

FRONT VIEW

- CLIENT
- BUDGET
- DEADLINE

NOTES

SIDE VIEW

TOP VIEW

MATERIAL COMPONENTS

MATERIALS	WEIGHT	QUANTITY	PRICE

PROJECT

FRONT VIEW

CLIENT

BUDGET

DEADLINE

NOTES

SIDE VIEW

TOP VIEW

MATERIAL COMPONENTS

MATERIALS	WEIGHT	QUANTITY	PRICE

PROJECT

FRONT VIEW

CLIENT

BUDGET

DEADLINE

NOTES

SIDE VIEW

TOP VIEW

MATERIAL COMPONENTS

MATERIALS	WEIGHT	QUANTITY	PRICE

PROJECT

FRONT VIEW

CLIENT

BUDGET

DEADLINE

NOTES

SIDE VIEW

TOP VIEW

MATERIAL COMPONENTS

MATERIALS	WEIGHT	QUANTITY	PRICE

PROJECT

FRONT VIEW

- CLIENT
- BUDGET
- DEADLINE

NOTES

SIDE VIEW

TOP VIEW

MATERIAL COMPONENTS

MATERIALS	WEIGHT	QUANTITY	PRICE

PROJECT

FRONT VIEW

CLIENT

BUDGET

DEADLINE

NOTES

SIDE VIEW

TOP VIEW

MATERIAL COMPONENTS

MATERIALS	WEIGHT	QUANTITY	PRICE

PROJECT

FRONT VIEW

CLIENT

BUDGET

DEADLINE

NOTES

SIDE VIEW

TOP VIEW

MATERIAL COMPONENTS

MATERIALS	WEIGHT	QUANTITY	PRICE

PROJECT

FRONT VIEW

CLIENT

BUDGET

DEADLINE

NOTES

SIDE VIEW

TOP VIEW

MATERIAL COMPONENTS

MATERIALS	WEIGHT	QUANTITY	PRICE

PROJECT

FRONT VIEW

CLIENT

BUDGET

DEADLINE

NOTES

SIDE VIEW

TOP VIEW

MATERIAL COMPONENTS

MATERIALS	WEIGHT	QUANTITY	PRICE

PROJECT

FRONT VIEW

- CLIENT
- BUDGET
- DEADLINE

NOTES

SIDE VIEW

TOP VIEW

MATERIAL COMPONENTS

MATERIALS	WEIGHT	QUANTITY	PRICE

PROJECT

FRONT VIEW

CLIENT

BUDGET

DEADLINE

NOTES

SIDE VIEW

TOP VIEW

MATERIAL COMPONENTS

MATERIALS	WEIGHT	QUANTITY	PRICE

PROJECT

FRONT VIEW

CLIENT

BUDGET

DEADLINE

NOTES

SIDE VIEW

TOP VIEW

MATERIAL COMPONENTS

MATERIALS	WEIGHT	QUANTITY	PRICE

PROJECT

FRONT VIEW

CLIENT

BUDGET

DEADLINE

NOTES

SIDE VIEW

TOP VIEW

MATERIAL COMPONENTS

MATERIALS	WEIGHT	QUANTITY	PRICE

PROJECT

FRONT VIEW

CLIENT

BUDGET

DEADLINE

NOTES

SIDE VIEW

TOP VIEW

MATERIAL COMPONENTS

MATERIALS	WEIGHT	QUANTITY	PRICE

PROJECT

FRONT VIEW

CLIENT

BUDGET

DEADLINE

NOTES

SIDE VIEW

TOP VIEW

MATERIAL COMPONENTS

MATERIALS	WEIGHT	QUANTITY	PRICE

PROJECT

FRONT VIEW

- CLIENT
- BUDGET
- DEADLINE

NOTES

SIDE VIEW

TOP VIEW

MATERIAL COMPONENTS

MATERIALS	WEIGHT	QUANTITY	PRICE

PROJECT

FRONT VIEW

- CLIENT
- BUDGET
- DEADLINE

NOTES

SIDE VIEW

TOP VIEW

MATERIAL COMPONENTS

MATERIALS	WEIGHT	QUANTITY	PRICE

PROJECT

FRONT VIEW

CLIENT

BUDGET

DEADLINE

NOTES

SIDE VIEW

TOP VIEW

MATERIAL COMPONENTS

MATERIALS	WEIGHT	QUANTITY	PRICE

PROJECT

FRONT VIEW

CLIENT

BUDGET

DEADLINE

NOTES

SIDE VIEW

TOP VIEW

MATERIAL COMPONENTS

MATERIALS	WEIGHT	QUANTITY	PRICE

PROJECT

FRONT VIEW

CLIENT

BUDGET

DEADLINE

NOTES

SIDE VIEW

TOP VIEW

MATERIAL COMPONENTS

MATERIALS	WEIGHT	QUANTITY	PRICE

PROJECT

FRONT VIEW

CLIENT

BUDGET

DEADLINE

NOTES

SIDE VIEW

TOP VIEW

MATERIAL COMPONENTS

MATERIALS	WEIGHT	QUANTITY	PRICE

PROJECT

FRONT VIEW

CLIENT

BUDGET

DEADLINE

NOTES

SIDE VIEW

TOP VIEW

MATERIAL COMPONENTS

MATERIALS	WEIGHT	QUANTITY	PRICE

PROJECT

FRONT VIEW

CLIENT

BUDGET

DEADLINE

NOTES

SIDE VIEW

TOP VIEW

MATERIAL COMPONENTS

MATERIALS	WEIGHT	QUANTITY	PRICE

PROJECT

FRONT VIEW

CLIENT

BUDGET

DEADLINE

NOTES

SIDE VIEW

TOP VIEW

MATERIAL COMPONENTS

MATERIALS	WEIGHT	QUANTITY	PRICE

PROJECT

FRONT VIEW

CLIENT

BUDGET

DEADLINE

NOTES

SIDE VIEW

TOP VIEW

MATERIAL COMPONENTS

MATERIALS	WEIGHT	QUANTITY	PRICE

PROJECT

FRONT VIEW

CLIENT

BUDGET

DEADLINE

NOTES

SIDE VIEW

TOP VIEW

MATERIAL COMPONENTS

MATERIALS	WEIGHT	QUANTITY	PRICE

PROJECT

FRONT VIEW

- CLIENT
- BUDGET
- DEADLINE

NOTES

SIDE VIEW

TOP VIEW

MATERIAL COMPONENTS

MATERIALS	WEIGHT	QUANTITY	PRICE

PROJECT

FRONT VIEW

CLIENT

BUDGET

DEADLINE

NOTES

SIDE VIEW

TOP VIEW

MATERIAL COMPONENTS

MATERIALS	WEIGHT	QUANTITY	PRICE

PROJECT

FRONT VIEW

CLIENT

BUDGET

DEADLINE

NOTES

SIDE VIEW

TOP VIEW

MATERIAL COMPONENTS

MATERIALS	WEIGHT	QUANTITY	PRICE

PROJECT

FRONT VIEW

CLIENT

BUDGET

DEADLINE

NOTES

SIDE VIEW

TOP VIEW

MATERIAL COMPONENTS

MATERIALS	WEIGHT	QUANTITY	PRICE

PROJECT

FRONT VIEW

- CLIENT
- BUDGET
- DEADLINE

NOTES

SIDE VIEW

TOP VIEW

MATERIAL COMPONENTS

MATERIALS	WEIGHT	QUANTITY	PRICE

PROJECT

FRONT VIEW

CLIENT

BUDGET

DEADLINE

NOTES

SIDE VIEW

TOP VIEW

MATERIAL COMPONENTS

MATERIALS	WEIGHT	QUANTITY	PRICE

www.ingramcontent.com/pod-product-compliance
Lightning Source LLC
Chambersburg PA
CBHW081231080526
44587CB00022B/3899